THE
GRIFFIN
POETRY
PRIZE
Anthology 2014

THE
GRIFFIN
POETRY
PRIZE
Anthology 2014

A SELECTION OF THE SHORTLIST

Edited by ROBERT BRINGHURST

ANANSI

This edition published in 2014 by
House of Anansi Press Inc.
110 Spadina Avenue, Suite 801
Toronto, ON, M5V 2K4
Tel. 416-363-4343
Fax 416-363-1017
www.houseofanansi.com

Distributed in Canada by
HarperCollins Canada Ltd.
1995 Markham Road
Scarborough, ON, M1B 5M8
Toll free tel. 1-800-387-0117

Distributed in the United States by
Publishers Group West
1700 Fourth Street
Berkeley, CA 94710
Toll free tel. 1-800-788-3123

House of Anansi Press is committed to protecting our natural environment.
As part of our efforts, the interior of this book is printed on paper made from
second-growth forests and is acid free.

18 17 16 15 14   1 2 3 4 5

Library and Archives Canada Cataloguing in Publication

Cataloguing data available from Library and Archives Canada

Library of Congress Control Number: 2014907275

Cover design: Chloé Griffin and Kyra Griffin
Cover image: Dirk Bell, Untitled, 2013, Pencil on Paper, 18.5 x 24.9 cm/
Photograph on inside front and back cover: Chloé Griffin
Photo Courtesy: BQ, Berlin
Typesetting: Jessica Mifsud

 Canada Council Conseil des Arts
for the Arts du Canada

 ONTARIO ARTS COUNCIL
CONSEIL DES ARTS DE L'ONTARIO

*We acknowledge for their financial support of our publishing program
the Canada Council for the Arts, the Ontario Arts Council, and the Government of Canada
through the Canada Book Fund.*

Printed and bound in Canada

CONTENTS

CANADIAN FINALISTS

PREFACE

I have been involved most of my life in the design and printing of books as well as in writing and reading them, but the Griffin Prize — to its everlasting credit — is awarded purely for poetry, not for design and presentation. So I embarked on reading the 539 books submitted to this year's jury with the expectation that I might sometimes have to hold my typographic nose. In fact my two co-jurors, C. D. Wright and Jo Shapcott, were no less interested than I in the physical properties of books, and the subject was mentioned a number of times in our telephonic deliberations. My nose, however, did not suffer. The overall typographic standard in English-language poetry books has risen a fair bit over the past dozen years — so if design had been one of the factors by which we judged these books, we would have tossed out few on that criterion alone.

Standards of copyediting and proofreading, however, appear to have fallen over the same span of time, and there are some howlers in several works on our shortlists. I noticed over twenty editorial slips in one of our three Canadian selections and a handful of sometimes hilarious blunders in two of the four books from our international shortlist. This is not, evidently, from lack of financial resources, for the publishers did not skimp on the physical production of these three titles. I mention these facts in the hope that readers, writers, and publishers will agree that better editing and proofing is worth everything it costs.

Two of the three Canadian finalists — Anne Carson's *Red Doc>* and Anne Michaels' *Correspondences* — are books in the ontological as well as physical sense of the word. That is to say, they are not collections of short lyrics but single, book-length poems, though each consists of many sections. An attempt to represent such works by printing excerpts — which it is my duty to do in this anthology — is guaranteed to fail. The book-length poem, like the novel, can reveal its true character only to those who read it entire. Two other books from our shortlists — Sue Goyette's *Ocean* and Tomasz Różycki's *Colonies* — are constructed as numbered sequences: 56 series of couplets in Goyette's case, and 77 sonnets in Różycki's. Here too there is an integrity to be found in reading the whole that cannot be replicated by any selection of parts.

These are not the only hurdles that make the anthologist's job both hazardous and interesting. A number of the poems in Brenda Hillman's book, *Seasonal Works with Letters on Fire*, include tiny photographs. These leap into the text like snapshots popping up unbidden on a cellphone, but they cannot be recopied like the words, nor can they be pronounced when one wishes to quote a few lines. Some of Hillman's poems also include short phrases in Portuguese, Arabic, and the Iranian language Dari. The Arabic and Dari clearly baffled her original publisher's typesetter and proofreader, and we have tried to correct their errors here.

Anne Carson's book, though steeped in Greek, is written in English only; and though it is poetry, it is written almost entirely in prose instead of verse. Most of that prose is set in very narrow, unhyphenated columns. Carson's highly sophisticated work therefore wallows in the atrocious justification that is typical of the world's least sophisticated newspapers. This is a typographic problem we as readers of the poem are clearly invited to share rather than solve. Carson's anticlassical columns, or pillars, of text are therefore carefully recreated in this anthology, warts and all.

Anne Michaels' poem presents a challenge of a different kind. It was originally published in a concertina binding — something rarely seen except in handmade limited editions. The poem occupies one side of a long, collapsible, sheet or folding scroll. On the other side are full-size colour reproductions of twenty-six small gouache portraits, painted by Bernice Eisenstein, of characters who are mentioned or alluded to in the poem. Here, necessarily, the excerpts from the poem are presented in conventional codex form and without the illustrations.

Incidentally, I have followed the same simple principle in representing each of the seven books. I allotted each author precisely twelve pages and chose complete poems (or complete sections of the book-length poems) that seemed to me readable in relative isolation. The pieces I chose are not always contiguous in the original publication, but they are still in a sequence chosen by the author. In other words, though much has been left out, the remaining parts have not been rearranged.

Tomasz Różycki's book is fully bilingual — as all editions of translated poetry ought to be. As jurors for the Griffin Prize, we were asked to assess this book on the merits of Mira Rosenthal's English translation alone. Yet the merits of any translation depend fundamentally on how it reflects and refracts the original. I have therefore included the Polish text of Różycki's poems, though not *en face*, which is how they appear in the shortlisted volume itself.

It is hard not to notice that translation — and the underlying multilingual nature of human history and society — has been crucially important to nearly every poet in this company. Różycki himself is a distinguished translator of French into Polish. Anne Carson is a celebrated scholar of classical Greek. Carl Phillips — whose beautifully written *Silverchest* shows how fruitfully he has read Catullus and Horace — made his living for some years by teaching Latin. Rachael Boast's book, *Pilgrim's Flower*, is threaded with variations on works by Cocteau and Rimbaud. Anne Michaels' poem is written against a background rich with German, French, and Yiddish, which at times invade her poem. Brenda Hillman's work, as I've mentioned, is laced with other languages too. So while we celebrate here the poetry being written in only one of humanity's languages, we are at the same time celebrating quite a bit more.

Robert Bringhurst
Quadra Island, 2 April 2014

INTERNATIONAL
FINALISTS

RACHAEL BOAST

Pilgrim's Flower

Rachael Boast's *Pilgrim's Flower* is remarkable for its intense lyricism, its metaphysical warmth and precision. Although Boast's poems do not depict life in any autobiographical sense, they do show us, perhaps more interestingly, a mind in action, a mind that connects with an electric charge to place, people, language. In "Double Life," a poem addressed to Thomas Chatterton, Boast speaks of "the mutable self fluttering by candlelight," a phrase which might serve as the key to her project: it is the lyric moment which offers a way of understanding the mutability of both the observer and the observed; it is the lyric moment which permits glimpses of the fluttering connection between. Other writers are evoked, too: Akhmatova and Coleridge are among those in conversation with the poet. The effect is to bring their writing, their thinking into the present moment for the reader, a kind of layered time-travel only the best lyric poems allow.

The layers of history also emerge in those poems, which look inside and outside the boundaries of place. The spiritual and the physical co-exist in the stones of the cathedral in "Caritas" just as they do in the sonnet in which they are held: "And what comes across, half-said / into all that space, is that it's enough / to love the air we move through."

Caritas

(St Andrews Cathedral)

These stones speak a level language
murmured word by word,
a speech pocked and porous with loss,
and the slow hungers of weathering.

And there, in the broken choir, children
are all raised voice, loving the play of outline
and absence where the dissembled god
has shared his shape and homed us.

At the end of the nave, the east front stands
both altered and unchanged,
its arch like a glottal stop.

And what comes across, half-said
into all that space, is that it's enough
to love the air we move through.

Cocteau Twins

I've heard the phrase *between you
and me* too many times to believe

it to be true, but between me and you
there was Cocteau, wagging his testimonial

finger, as usual, while flat out on the floor
with my arms in receipt of the flower

of thought, palms upwards, I envisaged
the inside eyes of his hands remaking words

for a song that is a drawing that is a film —
that is, a poem; and in the middle of all this

the books on the shelves float down while
falling upwards, slipping out of their jackets

as the naked petals of their pages turn
into mirrors, which is to say, they blossom.

Losing My Page

Nothing was ever straightforward with you
and so, instead of returning to where
I left off, I re-entered the poem
from afar — it hardly mattered where —

and eventually reached the same clearing
marked, I'd noticed, by the hands of time
held up in prayer, where I'd seen you before —
or thought I had — at the midnight hour

you rhyme yourself with. Page after page
the light would change, to dark and back again,
reminding me of someone who, when put

on the spot, knows the dance of gain and loss
by the secret fidelity of moving
from one foot to the other, to the other.

The Withdrawing Room

(7 Great George Street)

The seventh of ten bells on sprung-coils
outside the basement kitchen is rung
by a man in the upstairs drawing room.
Such is this house of servitude. So too,
the call sounded sometime before
for a young Devonian to drop in
one September afternoon in 1795.
Take this as *a repetition in the finite mind*
and in the sweetest way possible
he never actually materialized,
such are the echoes of this house of sugar.

But suppose that one man is reading aloud,
pacing the boards, up and down,
while another stares at the view
of the Cathedral's medieval tower
where, later, a marble bust of his own head
stands in a stellate alcove.
Which leaves a third man who,
absenting himself from the game
at play, is all the more animated
for having noticed a painting of the Avon Gorge
to which his back is now turned.

He's just seen how all things are cut
from the same rock, all things
a repeating echo of the mind of God.
Has seen, in the water,
an image of recollection, so much so
that everything looks inside out
and the ornate room — the bone china,
the house of cards on the soft tabletop —

will return one day to its prima materia
while we'd remember reality the more
by mirroring the long attention of the river.

After Sappho

On this dark earth
the night ambush at the blockades,
peace envoys in the arms trade,
operation Odyssey, the shock and the awe —
all these are an insult to the power of love.

Understand this, it's easy:
a thousand ships in pursuit of a woman —
who only wanted to hide her face
in one man's embrace —
stood no chance against the undertow

of love's will . . . Which brings me back to you.
How I too, overcoming the checkpoints
of the mind, slipped past the guards
with their yes or no answers, outwitted Mars
and went after you.

I carry in my heart this clannish chant
for a compass. And always
it knows where you are
just as you know, by the light of the stars,
that our love's a moon too new to be seen.

Milestones

What can Sappho's Leap have been beyond this?
　　—S. T. Coleridge

They had the map while you out-walked them,
so much so that at every inn they chanced on
you'd already spent the night,
drunk the wine and polished off
the oatcakes reserved for *strays*.

The misunderstandings were such
that after an evening of nervous laughter
at Loch Katrine, you were advised
to make your own way home. Soon as.
So instead, you went north

along the Great Glen Road,
regaining your liberty in burnt shoes;
across Wade's High Bridge
with the void in your stomach enlarged
by the long scope down to the Spean

where, slipshod and open to suggestion,
the journey falls into place:
on to the Moray Firth, your only map
the highs and lows of the landscape
opening in front of your eyes.

Aubade

In the emollient night of roses and paraffin,
of burning hands and of all that burns

of broken sleep piecing together what for
so long had remained lost of what was lost

not in the dark but in the fire of the dark
in the night and in the oil of the night

of everything you were led to believe in,
everything stays secret until — one morning —

you put your hands through the touch
of the unfinished light and took it back.

Tearing and Mending

*(the first three minutes and seven seconds of
"Hiroshima Mon Amour")*

After rewind and replay it's still unclear
how the burned skin of the embrace

flinches into intimacy, into focus,
then changes into dust, then rain;

the tenderness of love's erotesis,
the way her fingers press into the soft

of his back, into its folds and the otherness
of its give asking questions she can never

forget. He answers back, his body ablaze
with remembered dawns, each movement

of his mouth cracked with the fricative
of war; their torn hearts hiding the memory

of shadow and stone, transfigured
into rain, then dust, then flesh and bone.

Redressing Marsyas

For you I bring all the woodwinds
back out of the trees
to give music to your words,

the flutes and the reed pipes
buried under the pines
at a time when your expectations

were lower than anything on earth;
when the stories of this upside down world
would hide their true meaning

under the skin of the imagined,
the rind of fable,
no thanks to Ovid's tall tales —

for even Alcibiades, drunk out of his skull
in the lap of Socrates,
could see through the outward form

and find gods inside a hollow man;
and yet a sober man, for all his spin,
sees only what he wants to see:

air in a raw lung, or the twin arteries
of hubris and overstepping,
and whatever else suits his perversion.

The image alone of Marsyas,
metamorphosed
into the clearest river in Phrygia

by the grief-silver of his mourners
leaves me paying my respects
to what's always left unspoken;

that you deserve more than a gift
that didn't open, lost libretto
for a satyr who, in another life,

we see balancing a wine glass
on his upright phallus, his skin
unmarked, his hair and beard lush

as the tussocks of Olympus;
songs you tore to pieces
thinking the stakes were too high,

as if the music of chance
and the palace it led to
were meant for someone other than you.

Spring Tide

Tonight from the window the river's back-flow
borrows from an obscured moon,

new born, making the hours
become moments more than themselves

which perhaps is what time is for.
You've just left this edgeland

of everything that's out of our hands
even as it belongs to us; which is why

my face is as bright as water
thinking back to you for the sake of it

inwardly lit with a love of the weather
you bring here; this long calm like a path

we're guided down by the call
of an owl. Always so, it's always so.

BRENDA HILLMAN

Seasonal Works with Letters on Fire

Seasonal Works with Letters on Fire concludes Brenda Hillman's tetralogy on the four elements of classical thought. She steers wildly but ably through another day of teaching, a ceremonial equinox, the distress of bee colony collapse; space junk, political obstruction, military drones, administrative headaches, and everything in between. The "newt under the laurel" and "the herring purring through the eelgrass" don't escape her arc of acuity. *Seasonal Works* appears to be one of the most inclusive books a hyperactive imagination could wring out of the actual. The symbols of the alphabet come alive and perform acrobatic marvels. Phonetical birdcalls join in on cue. The mighty challenges of *now* are fully engaged. The book performs an "anarchic music" and stimulates a craving for undiluted love, and a rollicking fury for justice that only its widely variant forms can sustain. This is a unique work. Its letters are on fire.

At the Solstice, a Yellow Fragment

Our lord of literature
   visits my love,
they have gone below,
they have lost their way
among the tablets
of the dead —;

   preeeee — dark energy — woodrat
  in the pine, furred thing
     & the fine,
a suffering among syllables, stops
  winter drops from cold, cold,
miracle night (a fox
     deep in its hole under yellow
    thumbs of the chanterelles,
  (no: gold. Gold thumbs, Goldman Sachs
    pays no tax . . . (baby goats
in the pen, nor blaming God,
    not blaming them —

(alias: buried egg of the shallow-helmet turtle
    [*Actinemys marmorata*]
alias: thanks for calling the White House
    comment line))))

For your life had stamina
from a childhood among priests
& far in the night,
beyond the human realm, a cry
released the density of nature —

Between Semesters, the Fragments Follow Us

As a heron stalks the smart frog,
time stabs the mini-brenda
(we had a winter panic, then it grew —!)
Valved season, approaching Imbolc:
sounds of the newly dead
eee-^^eeyyy, your verbs do little flips
like Russian gymnasts —
thousands of herring purr
through the eelgrass [*Zostera*] with (at the end
of the middle of the end of empire) plastic
buoys, rope, Arabic bronze kelp washed up —
العربية take me too, present tense, take us,
driftwood, each aperture
so mongrel-sized . . .

Across Tomales, children merge with screens,
& farther in: pre-rectangles on the backs
of turtles; there is sexual laughter
in the dune grass —
over the shards, stars buckle
& wheel . . . Some of the fragments are lost,
Osiris. Your lover will find them
with her quantum style —

Equinox Ritual with Ravens & Pines

— so we said to the somewhat: Be born —
   & the shadow kept arriving in segments,
  cold currents pushed minerals
  up from the sea floor, up through
coral & labels of Diet Coke blame shame
    bottles down there —
  it is so much work to appear!

unreadable zeroes drop lamps
  as mustard fields [*Brassica rapa*]
gold without hinges, a vital
    echo of caring . . . On the census,
just write: *it exists!* Blue Wednesday
   bells strike the air like forks
  on a thrift store plate,
& the shadow moves off to the side . . .

In the woods, loved ones tramp through
  the high grass; they wait in a circle
   for the fire to begin;
they throw paper dreams & sins upon
    the pyre & kiss, stoking the first
  hesitant flame after touching a match
to the bad news — branches are thrust back
across myths before the flame catches —;
ravens lurch through double-knuckled
   pines & the oaks & the otherwise;
a snake slithers over serpentine
then down to the first
    dark where every cry has size —

   FOR EK & MS

To Leon, Born before a Marathon

When you were born,
they fell in love with sleep;
doves delivered the five wax notes;
a pointed moon brought in its radiance.
Some were strapping distance on their feet
as you cried out among the architectures;
month of the fiddlehead,
hounds-tongue, coltsfoot;
month of the normal rains —

& though earth is somewhat tired
of the new, there would never
not be news again. Tall wild stalks
circled the lake,
stirring shouting into the street,
a little gray trash scattered;
& when the runners finally passed,
rebel seeds had joined an auxiliary
race. You brought
two kinds of hours
into days; one kind was blank;
one had your expression on its face —

Fable of Work in the World

You threw your book in the ocean,
    a big wave hooked it
down through meaning,
up through noon;
      — why did you do that, sister?
      — chaos enchanted me, mister
        A plover stole the cover
        on a breezelet from the sea.

It's wild to give up your labor —;
wind shook the water like paper:
  half a fable, half an april
in a kingdom by the sea.
      — You stole that from Poe.
      — Did not.
      — Did too.
A big fish took it,
a halibut with a habitat —
  down to molting sea lions
& serpentine grains below.

It's hard to give up your labor
    but you never owned it, did you,
    nor did the volcano, the glad,
the flat, the red, sad miracle;
it burned between you & the reader
    who heard with an oval mind
      a reedy local music
      in a curved time.

    FOR GWF

Very Far Back in This Life

Rublev, the great painter of icons,
   is buried under one of his own churches;
infinity stretches in all directions. Under
      the bricks, he hears the carriages move.
Visitors from countries stand in the square;
    below their feet, the demons pass
back & forth between the worlds . . .

The icon watches as they are struck dumb
    by the brown facility of paint.
Color has lost its innocence.
     Russia is an enormous plain
        over which wild energy rides.
    Christ looks sickly & helpful,
raising two fingers. His eyes have apostrophes,
cloves of garlic. An artist is never your enemy.

How to interpret the painting through
   circles of violence that made it. It moves
      much more slowly than you do;
it always has something to conceal.
 A painting shows you how to breathe.
      History is still: it's the wood horse
burning on its side. A dome
sacrifices itself to a bell; its ringing
 swells & falls, a maybe yes
     & maybe no that follows you —

To the Writing Students at Orientation

This has certainly been an odd week. An earthquake in the East instead of the West. Rebels have taken Tripoli. A billionaire agreed to tax himself & then bought a bank. Astronomers have discovered a small planet composed, perhaps, of diamond. It is 4000 light years away, is about the size of Jupiter & it seems to have become a diamond by spinning around its companion, a pulsar, every few hours. Which brings us to your writing. Here you are; you've been told all your life you're too sensitive. Maybe you had trouble navigating details, yet you found your way to a room at the edge of a metropolis. You're calm or anxious now. What are you doing here? A red-tailed hawk circles the dry grass. Migrant birds come through for a few days, skimming the scrub brush for fuzzy food. Seeds of the Manzanita turn red. That locale is outside your head. The other locale, not yet named, is inside you. You fell in love with language early on, with certain words, with syntax. Though you had a worried childhood, this love of language held you & you have always enjoyed making forms from particular words & their order, you want to make them more compelling, strange or exact. But you are lonely with ideas; you came to this room because it is difficult to have consciousness in the twenty-first century, & you need a community, & here they possibly are, sitting beside you. Your writing has a social dimension in a culture often numb to art. Here are some lines from Hölderlin: "But the poet can't keep / His knowledge to himself and likes to join / With others, who help him understand it."

Out in the dark, the diamond planet orbits the companion star as art circles the unnamable. Why? It is the great task.

When the Occupations Have Just Begun

One style cannot complete the unknown.
    You cry before others in autumn,
      a nature you must repeat to live.
Friends comfort you as they pass.
    Obdurate cliffs drop into the sea
as tears pour from your heart's
       intricate oddity. Acid soil slides down
where anchovies spawn. A tender enigma
    shines in the clinging cypresses —;
    their roots recall the young hurt.

When people pitch tents in the streets
   their cries make earthquakes swell.
Rats & crows cross the fire zone
     to visit assemblies, *Danaus plexippus*
between lender & being lent.
    Violent & less violent turn
on the wheel of night. When generators
     vanish, squat candles are lit.
You cry as the wounded leave & return.
   So many years have failed to show
     what the unwanted wanted
to undo. You're told to stay calm,
    be reasonable & wait,
transfixed as you are by the public sphere
     but your body has been very
  very reasonable so far,
your body is the archive of the world —

    FOR LD

& the Tents Went Back Up

They were not begging protection
from Achilles. They were not
the upper tent on the insular beach.
They were not stable or accurate, had not
been carried on heads like buckets. Anti-tent,
the intent. People pledged fire
in them, they were not groundless
as settlers' cloth, they had no ticking grease.
They were full of autochthonous tones,
a hawk, an owl, a raven screech.
The poor & the great dead set them up,
they were geometrical. St. Hildegard's tent
of eyes. When a girl reads in a mountainous
tent, her flashlight makes triangles
without sides. Tent of the Bedouin
where sand is perfect speech. Threads
are pitched as future tents,
abstract & not, pure as experience. You sit
with others in the sexual dark. The tent
that keeps the starlight safe
doesn't care for the wrong law.
The visible is frayed; starlight streams
into you, wild & invisible.
The invisible is unafraid.

An Almanac of Coastal Winter Creatures

    — & an owl makes consonants
  between the categories; a heart
protects itself against the State.
   Fog seeps through extra fog
while sea lions drape on rocks
like carpet samples. Just off
   freeway ramps, bad loans
      not gone. Come, profit,
    let us repair to the living room
where we'll break up with you.
   Needles of sun pierce
the winter pears. Oh, even opened
     the bay laurel . . . Oh, even
opened the silky tassel *Garrya elliptica* —

   Meaning presses in from the unknown
to rooms where we read in our damaged skin.
    We bring our sexual dreams
at dawn. Thrushes
   appear all Braille in vests driving
     verbs from the hazel. *Corylus*
cornuta, puffy puff-puff, so late. The heart
   can hear in diastolic rest; the heart
   protects itself against the State.
In my dream, we got into the train.
    Our coast had broken off &
  pulled the occupation on a string;
i asked if you brought the map;
   you said you had
   evidence of where we'd been —

The Second Half of the Survey

They come to your office
with winking tablets on fire,
  they bring threads from the legend,
they wear black, they don't
      decline the death talk.
You are tired. Spring revises
its history. On a cliff, the new calf
      stands after an hour. On a tower
of ruptured stone, the worm crawls
      through a sentence — if you
could take your strength, like that!

      Our lord of literature
obliquely rests
  like a dancer in her box
of limits — most everything no human
eye shall see —:
      an "if only"! immeasurable —

The student sits before you
      reading aloud, & when
  the letters have recovered, they make
a blind doctrine of sequence. Meaning
  is their Caliban, a search
      removed from history. Phenomena
  request your attention: out the window:
      an ecstasy of now —

In the Evening of the Search

Vastness of dusk, after a day —
    what is a person? Too late
to ask this now. The court has ruled
    a corporation is a person.
Persons used to be called souls.
    On the avenue, a lucky person
stands in a convenience store
    scratching powder from his ticket —
silver flecks fall from his thumbs
    to galaxies below.

        Deep in the night
    a trough of chaos forms;
your lover's body stops it every time.
    Meteors of the season over minnows
in the creek with two kinds of crayfish,
    tiny mouths & claws
        — nervous, perfect, perfect
life — the flesh of a dreamer,
    facing the wall —

    Around each word you're reading
there spins the unknowable flame.
        When you wake, a style
of world shakes free
    from the dream. It doesn't stop
        when you go out;
it doesn't stop when you come back
    as you were meant to —

CARL PHILLIPS

Silverchest

Carl Phillips is a poet of the line and a poet of the sentence, both at once. Rubbing these two intangible structures — one musical, the other linguistic — against one another is an ancient way of kindling verbal and intellectual fire, and Phillips does it in poem after poem with casual mastery. The lines are carved in low relief, shaped by internal assonance, not by end-rhyme, while the sentences trace a perfectly grammatical yet occasionally dizzying switch-back trail, using the standard resources of prose to climb far beyond the prosaic domain. Phillips' *Silverchest* consists in large part of reflections on a love affair gone bad. It is a gay male love affair in this case, but the anguish, the self-doubt, the sense of abandonment and loss, are captured here with a tenderness, depth, and precision that can dance through sociocultural fences as easily as deer can dance across the grass. *Silverchest* speaks, as great books do, out of its own profound particularity, to and for something wordless and shared by us all.

Just the Wind for a Sound, Softly

There's a weed whose name I've meant all summer
to find out: in the heat of the day, dangling pods hardly
worth the noticing; in the night, blue flowers . . . It's as if
a side of me that he'd forgotten had forced into the light,
briefly, a side of him that I'd never seen before, and now
I've seen it. It is hard to see anyone who has become
like your own body to you. And now I can't forget.

Now Rough, Now Gentle

Never mind the parts that came later, with all
the uselessness, as usual, of hindsight: regret's
what it has to be, in the end, in which way it is
like death, any bowl of sliced-fresh-from-the-tree
stolen pears, this body that stirs,

                           or fails to, as I
turn away, meaning *Make it yours*, or *Hold tight*,
or *I begin to think maybe you were right — that
there's nothing, after* . . . though whether or not like
one of those moments just past having woken to
yet another stranger,

                      how the world can seem
to have completely stopped when, finally, it's just
a stillness — who can say? First I envied them,
then I came to love them for it, how the stars each
day become again invisible, while going nowhere.

Flight of Doves

I have been the king for whom the loveliest beasts
were slaughtered and turned trophy. I've seen how
brutality becomes merely the rhythm to a kind of
song to sing while bearing the light steadily forward,
the light in panels, in the shape that luck mostly takes

before a life comes true again: the room no different
than I remember leaving it: the snow still falls into it,
on the same man bound naked to a chair, and trembling,
saying *Take me* — meaning what, though, or where? — as
I brush the snow from his hair, as I take him, in my arms.

Surrounded as We Are, Unlit, Unshadowed

Squalor of leaves. November. A lone
hornets' nest. Paper wasps. Place where
everything that happens is as who says it will,
because. As in *Why shouldn't we have
come to this, why not*, this far, this
close to
        that below-zero where we almost
forget ourselves, rise at last unastonished
at the wreckery of it, what the wreckage
somedays can seem all along to have
been mostly, making you wonder what fear
is for, what prayer is, if not the first word
and not the last one either, if it changes
nothing of what you are still, black stars,
black
        scars, crossing a field that you've
crossed before, holding on, tight, though
careful, for you must be careful, so easily
torn is the veil diminishment comes
down to as it lifts and falls, see it falling,
now it lifts again, why do we love, at all?

First You Must Cover Your Face

There's a handful of black bees fastened
to the crepe myrtle's shot, all-but-gone-to-seed
flowers. Is it days, really, or only moments ago
that I almost told you everything,
before remembering what that leads
or has led to? How still they are — the bees, I mean,
not the flowers bending and unbending beneath
a rain that's come suddenly and, just as suddenly,
has stopped falling . . . Stillness, not of death,
but intoxication,
sweet coma,
zero-ness of no more wanting,
nothing left to want for, the meadow at last
fills with light, like a bowl,
filled with light, spilling with it, only harder now,
as if more desperate maybe, or just a thing that's brave.

Black Swan on Water, in a Little Rain

Seen this way,
through that lens where need
and wanting swim at random

toward each other, away again, and
now and then together, he moves less like
a swan — black, or otherwise — than like any

man for whom sex is, or has at last become,
an added sense by which to pass ungently but more
entirely across a life where, in between the silences,

he leaves what little he's got to show for himself
behind him in braids of water, green-to-blue wake of
Please and *Don't hurt me* and *You can see I'm hurt, already.*

My Meadow, My Twilight

Sure, there's a spell the leaves can make, shuddering,
and in their lying suddenly still again — flat, and still,
like time itself when it seems unexpectedly more
available, more to lose therefore, more to love, or
try to . . .

      But to look up from the leaves, remember,
is a choice also, as if up from the shame of it all,
the promiscuity, the seeing-how-nothing-now-will-
save-you, up to the wind-stripped branches shadow-
signing the ground before you the way, lately, all
the branches seem to, or you like to say they do,
which is at least half of the way, isn't it, toward
belief — whatever, in the end, belief

                          is . . . You can
look up, or you can close the eyes entirely, making
some of the world, for a moment, go away, but only
some of it, not the part about hurting others as the one
good answer to being hurt, and not the part that can
at first seem, understandably, a life in ruins, even if —
refusing ruin, because you

                  can refuse — you look
again, down the steep corridor of what's just another
late winter afternoon, dark as night already, dark
the leaves and, darker still, the door that, each night,
you keep meaning to find again, having lost it, you had
only to touch it, just once, and it bloomed wide open . . .

The Difference between Power and Force

In the east country where I must have lived once,
or how else remember it, the words came falling to
every side of me, words from a life that I'd thought,
if not easy, might at least be possible, though that
was then: *little crown* and *little burst of arrows*

and *ritual, loyalty, they are not the same* . . . I lay
rippling like a field shot through with amethyst
and reason. Then it seemed I myself was the field,
the words fell toward, then into me, each one no
sooner getting understood, than it touched the ground.

Darkness Is as Darkness Does

All night long, he's been a music almost
too far away to hear, and the man who
thinks he hears something that could maybe
be music: bits of flourish where there can't
or shouldn't be. As when camouflage matters
suddenly less than stillness. *Nothing in this world
like being held*, he says, turning away, meaning

I should hold him . . . I have been to Rome,
I have known the body, I have watched it fall,

and the green, green grass. How the deer re-
unsettled themselves across it, disproportionately
clumsy, for when they ran, there was grace. Then
the dream dog emerging again — hindquarters
first, as if dragging a great heaviness finally free
from the stand of trees that swayed, for a while,
the way bamboo does. Then silver birches.

Shimmer

He'd have drowned, without me. The eyes
stay shut. The mouth spills
      slightly open. The lips
move, or the snow's movement makes them
seem to, I can't tell. The gulls huddle as they
will, in a storm, the snow
         not so much settling on
as hovering about them, the wind in sudden gusts
lifting their feathers,
      then the feathers finding again
those positions that make flight, for a time, look
possible. When did souvenirs of what happened start
becoming tokens of what
        could have been becomes
one of those questions that, more and more, I keep
forgetting to stop asking. Now the snow seems a minor
chord; now a form of mercy — making
         less hard the edges
of what's hard. What's the point, in asking?
Why not rest my head upon the mirror that his chest is?

Anyone Who Had a Heart

I know a man who routinely asks
that I humiliate him. It's sex, and it isn't —
whatever. For him, it's a need, the way
brutality can seem for so long a likely
answer, that
        it becomes the answer —
a kindness, even, and I have always
been kind, for which reason it goes
against my nature to do what he says, but
there's little in nature that won't, with
enough training, change . . .
        After it's done,
if the weather's good, we tour his garden:
heliotrope, evening primrose . . . *Proximity's*
one thing, he likes to say, *penetration*
another, and I have learned that's true,
though which is better depends: whose life?
what story? the relief
        of snowmelt,
or the flooded fields again? We go down
to the stables to visit the horses that,
when they were nothing, just shivering
foals still, he once asked me to give
names to. How long we've traveled,
he and I — more like
        drifted, really — and
how far. More black than all the sorrows
and joys put together that I can remember
when I try remembering, which I mostly don't,
now the foals,
        they're stallions. Call out
Fanfare, Adoration. Like broken kings,
they lower their heads, then raise them.

But Waves, They Scatter

From beneath the ice field, longing looks up at the lovers
who — variously meandering, stalling or not, fucking
or not — guess nothing of him. Torturer sometimes. Known
also to have been a savior eventually, hard passage to a life
worth the hardness. You would think longing lived in a space
warmer than an ice field, you would think so. Tragedies are
happening everywhere in the world, beside things that aren't
technically tragedies, though they include suffering, pain, death
in its more humiliating versions, to remind that some of us
will be less spared, and some will not. Up through the ice field,
longing watches the lovers who, in turn, look down, or away,
laughing. Each time, they miss the ice field for the flowers that,
despite the cold, somehow grow there: distraction's the bluer
and more abundant flower, black at the edges. Joy is the other.

TOMASZ RÓŻYCKI

MIRA ROSENTHAL

Colonies

The sonnet, or "small song," arose in 13th-century Italy. It was successfully transplanted into English, through the supple voice of Thomas Wyatt, well before the birth of William Shakespeare. In Eastern Europe, however, the sonnet flowered much later. In Polish in particular, when it finally took hold, it met both popular acclaim and stiff-necked critical resistance. So the sonnet in Polish is, or can be, even now, a contentious and lively form. Tomasz Różycki's sonnet sequence *Kolonie* (*Colonies*), first published in Polish in 2006, demonstrates this clearly. In Mira Rosenthal's translation of this work, English-speaking readers can themselves confront the sonnet as something supple, fresh and a little bit strange. Różycki's quirky and self-deprecating humour permeates the poems. So does his sense of the fundamental homelessness of 21st-century human beings. Nine of these seventy-seven sonnets begin with some variation on the line "When I began to write, I didn't know . . ." and blossom into wry and hilarious reflections on the writing life. Others exude a heart-rending nostalgia for a world that is constantly being translated from meaning into money, and thus constantly destroyed.

2. Creoles, Mestizos

Since it is lucky you are strange and I
am strange, together we will shock the world.
Families strolling by will stare and point,
and we'll be famous, quite mysterious.

They'll even make up complicated plots
in films about us, all untrue. At night,
in mid-December, we will find ourselves
a hiding place where we'll make love and have

no other worries. We were meant to meet
in such a huge world, we are singled out
by language. Stick out your tongue for me, kitten.
I'll tell you a story. Luckily we're

together now, but language will betray us
and kill our world, turn it to dew and ash.

2. Kreole, metysi

Skoro ty jesteś dziwna i ja jestem dziwny,
to się wspaniale składa, razem zadziwimy
świat, będą pokazywać nas palcem rodziny
wychodzące na spacer, staniemy się słynni

i bardzo tajemniczy, nakręcą też filmy
o nas, zupełnie nieprawdziwe. Wprowadzimy
się w nocy, w środku grudnia do pewnej meliny
i będziemy tam robić miłość i nie będzie innych

spraw ani zajęć. Przyszło nam się spotkać
w takim ogromnym świecie, można nas rozpoznać
jedynie po języku. Pokaż język, kotku.
Opowiem ci bajeczkę. Będziemy już razem,

tak się wspaniale składa, i język nas zdradzi,
świat zabije, zamieni na rosę i popiół.

3. The Storm

At night three elements enjoy our bodies.
Fire, water, air. One moment you're water
then air the next, but flame encircles all.
At night we are reduced, small bits of tar,

soot on our skin, in cups. A storm enters
the room and clouds the mirror. There are others
from far away who look on us as food,
they eat and drink. They find each orifice

and enter us. Our bodies then become
the final element of earth and turn
to ash, dust, coal, compost where insects live
and snails leave tracks you ask about at dawn.

Once, at the world's end, I threw a stone into
the open mouth of hell; I can't complain.

3. Burza

W nocy naszych ciał używają trzy żywioły.
Ogień, woda, powietrze. Raz ty jesteś woda,
a raz jesteś powietrze, ale wokół pożar.
W nocy nas obracają, drobne kłaczki smoły,

sadzy na skórze, w kubku. Wchodzi do pokoju
burza i mąci lustra. Uznają za pokarm
nasze ciała też inni, którzy tu z daleka
przyszli, jedzą i piją. Znajdują otwory,

żeby w nie wejść. Nasze ciała stają się w nocy
czwartym żywiołem, ziemią, zmieniają się w popiół
i kurz, węgiel, próchnicę. Żyją w niej owady,
ślimaki robią ślady. Pytasz o to rano.

Kiedyś, na końcu świata sam wrzuciłem kamień
w otwarte usta piekła, nie mogę się skarżyć.

11. Headwinds

When I began to write, I didn't know
each of my words would bit by bit remove
things from the world and in return leave blank
spaces. That poems would begin to take

the place of my own homeland, mother, father,
first love, and second youth, and what I write
would fade from this world, trade its solid being
for unstable existence, turn to air,

wind, tremors, fire. And what my poems touch on
would freeze in life and crumble into small
particles, nearly turn to antimatter,
completely invisible dust, spinning

in the air a long time, till finally falling
into your eye, making it start to water.

11. Przeciwne wiatry

Kiedy zacząłem pisać, nie wiedziałem jeszcze,
że każde moje słowo będzie zabierało
po kawałku ze świata, w zamian zostawiając
jedynie miejsca puste. Ze powoli wiersze

zastąpią mi ojczyznę, matkę, ojca, pierwszą
miłość i drugą młodość, a co zapisałem
ubędzie z tego świata, zamieni swe stałe
istnienie na byt lotny, stanie się powietrzem,

wiatrem, dreszczem i ogniem, i to, co poruszę
w wierszu, znieruchomieje w życiu, i pokruszy
się na tak drobne cząstki, że się stanie prawie
antymaterią, pyłem, całkiem niewidzialnym

wirującym w powietrzu, tak długo, aż wpadnie
w końcu tobie do oka, a ono załzawi.

39. Coral Bay

When I began to write, I didn't know
how quickly it would make me very rich,
how I would buy an island and then fly
there fifteen times a day, how waves would place

old bottles at my feet, and narwhals from
those waves would eat straight from my hand, how my
nation would stretch to one-fifth of the world,
how I would bring home shells instead of pay,

and in the morning I'd discover precious
stones in the sheets, but I'd be just the same.
My pockets would be full of holes. I'd sit
with you as always at the table while

right there my women, children, livestock, land
would dance, rise in the air, then fall again.

39. Koralowa zatoka

Kiedy zacząłem pisać, nie wiedziałem wcale,
że się przez to tak szybko stanę tak bogaty,
że kupię sobie wyspę i będę tam latał
piętnaście razy dziennie, że będą mi fale

przynosiły butelki, że w falach nerwale
będą jadły mi z ręki, że piątą część świata
obejmie moje państwo, że zamiast wypłaty
będę przynosił muszle, że budząc się ranem

będę znajdował w łóżku szlachetne kamienie
i nic nie będzie po mnie widać. I kieszenie
będę miał wciąż dziurawe, będę z wami siadał
przy stole tak, jak zwykle, a moje kobiety,

dzieci, zwierzęta, ziemie przede mną w powietrzu
będą tańczyć, wznosić się, to znowu opadać.

49. Shamans

Mistral, sirocco, tramontane, and bora —
all names of demons written on the wings
of death's-head moths. Cézanne, Matisse, Derain,
tobacco, wine, all antidotes for sun

that starts its march at eight, its white tongue creeping
through vineyards. Look, and it will burn into
your world a black and blazing hole where faces
and names, birds, cities, years vanish. Each dawn

I see the fiery sword slash through a fish,
extract the milky spine. We sit here by the sea,
us three, tobacco, wine. I say, we're on vacation,
diving in waves, and time is a pearl unsheathed,

extracted from the oyster's chest. Just shut your eyes —
a colored state of grace. But he says, No, we're dead.

49. Szamani

Mistral i sirocco, tramontane, bora — imiona demonów
spisane na skrzydle ćmy, tej z trupią główką. Cezanne,
Matisse, Derain, czarny tytoń i wino, antidotum
dla słońca, które tu zaczyna o ósmej swój marsz,

przez winnice pełznie jego biały język. Kto na nie
popatrzy, wypali mu w świecie czarną płonącą
dziurkę, w którą będą wpadać twarze i imiona,
ptaki, miasta, lata. Widzę je co rano jak ognistym

mieczem rozpruwa rybę morza i wyjmuje mleczny
jej kręgosłup. Siedzimy we trzech, blisko wody,
czarny tytoń, wino. Ja mówię, że to wakacje,
nurkowanie w falach, że czas to perła, wyjęta

z pochwy, ze szkatułki ostrygi. Że kolory się stają
od zamknięcia powiek. On mówi, że to śmierć.

50. L'intérieur

Those nights, I took the metro. Faces that I thought
I knew from yellowed photographs got on,
but names and languages they spoke escaped me.
Faces got on, got off, women, kids, those

from home or farther, Armenians, Jews,
and soldiers from the three defeated armies.
Each told a story, youth, betrayal, towns
and neighbors, Europe. Each held close an object,

some vital evidence: a rusty medal,
a button from a grave, an eagle cap, a book
saved from a burning house, a lock of hair,
a letter from another world, a watch

stopped at farewell, that kiss which turns it all
to stone, all, even people, even air.

50. Interior

*Nocą jeździłem metrem. Ci, którzy wsiadali, mieli
twarze mi znane z żółtych fotografii, ale nie znałem
imion, ani języków, jakimi przemawiali. Na każdej
stacji wsiadali, wysiadali, dzieci i kobiety,*

*ci z rodziny i z dalszej, Ormianie i Żydzi, i żołnierze
w mundurach trzech rozbitych armii, i każdy opowiadał
historię o pięknej młodości, o zdradzie i miasteczku,
sąsiadach i Europie, i każdy miał jakiś przedmiot,*

*niezwykle istotny dowód: guzik wyjęty z grobu,
zardzewiały medalik, czapkę z orzełkiem, książkę
wyniesioną z płonącego mieszkania, kosmyk włosów
dziecka, list z innego świata, zepsuty zegarek,*

*który się zatrzymał w momencie pożegnania, kiedy
pocałunek zamienia w kamień wszystko, i ludzi, i wiatr.*

53. Scorched Maps

For J.B.

I took a trip to Ukraine. It was June.
I waded in the fields, all full of dust
and pollen in the air. I searched, but those
I loved had disappeared below the ground,

deeper than decades of ants. I asked
about them everywhere, but grass and leaves
have been growing, bees swarming. So I lay down,
face to the ground, and said this incantation —

you can come out, it's over. And the ground,
and moles and earthworms in it, shifted, shook,
kingdoms of ants came crawling, bees began
to fly from everywhere. I said come out,

I spoke directly to the ground and felt
the field grow vast and wild around my head.

53. Spalone mapy

Dla J.B.

*Pojechałem na Ukrainę, to był czerwiec
i szedłem po kolana w trawach, zioła i pyłki
krążyły w powietrzu. Szukałem, lecz bliscy
schowali się pod ziemią, zamieszkali głębiej*

*niż pokolenia mrówek. Pytałem się wszędzie
o ślady po nich, ale rosły trawy, liście,
i pszczoły wirowały. Kładłem się więc blisko,
twarzą na ziemi i mówiłem to zaklęcie —*

*możecie wyjść, już jest po wszystkim. I ruszała
się ziemia, a w niej krety i dżdżownice, i drżała
ziemia i państwa mrówek roiły się, pszczoły
latały ponad wszystkim, mówiłem wychodźcie,*

*mówiłem tak do ziemi i czułem, jak rośnie
trawa ogromna, dzika wokół mojej głowy.*

57. Old Fortress

The twentieth century's come to an end
and literature has left the cities,
their warm ashes, forgotten rooms, vast churches,
voices in cellars, cherry trees, the days before

graduation, archeology, and Germans,
Jews, Poles, and crowds at stations. Schulz is dead,
and Roth. From now on, literature has departed
these phantom gardens, districts, streets, has shed

its uniform and settled in the void,
where from the start its place has always been.
At last it's moved to weighty libraries,
virtual archives in machines. Brodsky

is dead, Mandelstam, Leśmian. It's joined
the depths, lost letters, pictures, dreams, nowhere.

57. Stara twierdza

*Skończył się wiek dwudziesty i literatura
opuściła już miasta, ich ciepłe popioły,
zapomniane pokoje, głębokie kościoły,
głosy w piwnicach, wiśnie i dni przed maturą,*

*archeologię i Niemców, Żydów, Polaków i tłumy
na dworcach. Umarł Szulz, Roth umarł. Od tej pory
literatura porzuciła już upiory
ulic, dzielnic, ogródków, zrzuciła mundury*

*i zamieszkała w pustce, tam, gdzie jest jej miejsce
od zawsze, od początku. Przeniosła się wreszcie
do ciężkiej biblioteki, do archiwum plików
wirtualnej maszyny. Umarli już Brodski,*

*Mandelsztam i Leśmian, i wstąpiła w otchłań,
do zagubionych listów, zdjęć, do snów, donikąd.*

60. Cannibals

When I began to write, I didn't know
who would be waiting for it. In the window,
a curtain hangs unmoved, a mess spreads on the floor:
loose change, CDs, an unmade bed, the entrails

of night. Signs of a struggle, deserted.
Someone left traces on these cups, this carpet,
someone bled out from self-inflicted wounds,
signed his name backwards, backwards. At this mirror,

a face, a face bit someone, a world leapt
from the other side, whole, identical
but in reverse. It occupied the best
places tonight and settled back to rest,

and no one sees it's false. Winter comes slowly,
frost pricks the window, pricks it and draws blood.

60. Ludożercy

Kiedy zacząłem pisać, jeszcze nie wiedziałem,
kto na to będzie czekać. Jest firanka w oknie
nieporuszona, bałagan w pokoju, drobne
pieniądze na podłodze, płyty, rozgrzebane

łóżko, wnętrzności nocy. Ślady walki, pusto.
Ktoś tu sobie zadawał rany, ktoś zostawił
ślady na szklankach, na dywanie, ktoś tu krwawił
i się podpisał wstecz, wstecz. Kogoś przed tym lustrem

ukąsiła ta twarz, twarz, cały świat wyskoczył
z tamtej strony, gotowy, niby identyczny,
ale przecież odwrotny i zajął tej nocy
tu odpowiednie miejsca, tu się usadowił

i nikt nie widzi fałszu. Powoli nadchodzi
zima i mróz nakłuwa wszystkie okna, do krwi.

68. Opium

When I began to write, I didn't know
that it's so simple. Just embrace it and
there's tools, there's ink. That there'd be different kinds
of pain, pain like a needle, white page pain.

That there'd be many pleasures, too, pleasure
like a needle, bliss of white page. And still
I didn't know I'd find these throbbing points
in you, on the sky's skin, and underground

where rivers flow. Just touch these points and it
will be, so primal, primal. Back then I didn't know
how easy it would be to write without memory,
head over heels, mad, fevered, with your whole

soul, more than life itself pining. And if I speak
with language, but don't know this, I'm nothing.

68. Opium

*Kiedy zacząłem pisać, nie wiedziałem jeszcze,
jakie to proste. Że wystarczy przylgnąć i znajdzie się
narzędzie, znajdzie się atrament, będą różne rodzaje bólu,
będzie ból jak igła i ból biała kartka, i że będzie*

*również wiele przyjemności przyjemność jak igła,
rozkosz jak biała kartka. Nie wiedziałem ciągle,
że znajdą się takie pulsujące punkty, w tobie,
na skórze nieba, będą też głęboko pod ziemią,*

*tam gdzie płyną rzeki, i że wystarczy ich dotknąć
i stanie się samo, jakie to zwierzęce, jakie to zwierzęce.
Nie wiedziałem wtedy, że tak łatwo pisać bez pamięci,
pisać do szaleństwa, gorąco, pisać całą duszą,*

*nad życie pisać, bez pisania uschnąć, i że byłbym niczym,
gdybym umiał mówić językami, a tego bym nie znał.*

71. Dolphins

When I began to write, I didn't know
that I would die. Since there was no death yet,
the human race lived in an age of gold,
metallic fragrance filled the streets. When I

began to write, I didn't know that the map ends
and the world's edge is guarded by a monster,
waves, ships, dolphins washing into its jaws.
That every night death takes my measurements,

collects stray hairs, the clippings from my nails,
my flaked-off skin and fashions for itself
a face like mine. That when death comes, this I
will be an anti-I. When I began to write,

I didn't know the subject would be death,
that I'd crumble to letters, soot, and toxic dust.

71. Delfiny

Kiedy zacząłem pisać, nie wiedziałem jeszcze,
że umrę. Ponieważ nie było jeszcze śmierci,
ludzkość żyła w wieku ze złota i na ulicach
czuć było w powietrzu metal. Kiedy zacząłem pisać,

nie wiedziałem wcale, że mapa gdzieś się kończy
i na skraju świata wije się ten potwór, do którego
paszczy wlewa się ocean, statki i delfiny.
Że śmierć będzie ze mnie brać co nocy miarę

i zbierać po mnie wypadłe włosy, paznokcie
i złuszczoną skórę, i że z tego będzie swą twarz
czynić na moje podobieństwo, i że kiedy nadejdzie,
to będę anty-ja. Kiedy zacząłem pisać,

nie wiedziałem jeszcze, że piszę właśnie o tym,
że się tak rozpadam na tysiące literek, sadzę, trujący pył.

76. The Governor's Residence

For J.P.

When I began to write, I didn't know
what I was really choosing and how much
they'd pay, that I'd become so quickly rich,
that anything I'd want could soon be mine —

the women and the cities of my dreams.
That I would travel when and where I want,
in winter or in summer, go where I
happen to point to on the map, without

a suitcase, straight from bed, without my pants.
I'd settle in a fishing hut in Greece,
and someone would bring wine and olives daily.
And day by day my fortune would increase,

and daily I'd stock up on chocolate, butter
that would sit there, for I would feel no hunger.

76. Dom gubernatora

Dla J.P.

Kiedy zacząłem pisać, wcale nie wiedziałem,
co naprawdę wybieram, ile za to płacą
i że w tak krótkim czasie stanę się bogaty,
i jeśli czegoś zechcę, zaraz to dostanę.

Moje będą kobiety, o jakich zamarzę,
i moje wszystkie miasta, pojadę na wczasy
gdziekolwiek tylko zechcę, zimą albo latem,
tam, gdzie wskażę na mapie, bez żadnych bagaży,

prosto z łóżka, bez spodni. Zamieszkam na skale
w rybackim domku w Grecji, i ktoś się postara
o wino i oliwki. I tak będzie co dnia.
I codziennie fortuna moja będzie wzrastać,

i co dzień nakupuję czekolady, masła,
i to będzie tak leżeć, bo nie będę głodny.

CANADIAN

FINALISTS

ANNE CARSON

Red Doc>

Red Doc>, Anne Carson's return to the characters of *Autobiography of Red*, stands on its own columns with pedestals in the fragments of Stesichorus' account of Herakles' final labor — to steal the red cattle of the monster Geryon. The narration puts the gaps to task. What is taken up again, more significantly than an update of *Autobiography*, is a daunting writer having her particular way with the language. Amid marvels of toaster-sized ice bats, barn-sized crows, and a silver-tuxedoed Hermes in humanlike form, is a dying mother's request of the daughter to pluck the hairs from her chin. Geryon returns middle-aged, Herakles, a damaged war veteran. Sexual bent is irrelevant; nature outsized, glacial and volcanic. Words are rescued, morphed and slapped awake. Speech hurtles from vulgar to sublime. Everything accelerates except when a break is introduced disguised as riff, list or song and the mead is served in golden cups.

TYPICAL NIGHT-HERDING SONGS gallop their rhythms and tell of love. G doesn't usually sing to the herd at night. He may talk to them listen stand in the herd. Listen. That community. A low purple listening but with a height to the sound. Them listening. They direct it up and out. They stand in a circle facing away from the center (calves in the center) and the long guard hairs hang down to brush their ankles like pines. Like queens. Like queens dressed in pines. Musk oxen are not in fact oxen not castrated bulls nor do their glands produce musk. Much is misnomer in our present way of grasping the world. But pines do always seem queenly as they sway so grand and anciently from the sky to the ground. Motion is part of listening. As the night goes on let's say he's there for a number of hours the motion changes. At first they just shudder a bit like any large entity come to rest but gradually imperially they begin swaying. Then as one rhythm they pass the sway from shape to shape around the circle its amplitude increasing its warmth rising from knees to hearts to eyes its pressures rolling across the large loose joints of the shoulders and down the long bones of the hips until at some point with a phrasing as simple as a perfect aphorism one of them spins up off its shanks and performs a 360-degree spin in air and returns to place. Slotting itself into the undulation of the others as firmly as *temptation* into *I can resist anything but.* He slips from thought to thought. Wilde Wild Wildness does surely attract him although what he knows about it is not much. Knows (with the oxen) that they prefer common gorse to willow shoots and can balance the topheaviness of their bodies by plaiting their feet as they walk. While with Sad he knows don't mention warplay.

Funny word warplay. Never says war or warfare. I've seen a lot of warplay he'd say. Warplay had me pumped those years. Tip of the spear. Flipswitch inside. She hit the ground 75 saw the white bag 75 bullets tore her head off I saw her hand. I wasn't going to tell anyone back home about. Oh it found its way out it surfaced. I had a tan when I came home no wounds no cuts. Everyone kissed me. Sure I sat by the fire I talked to the old man. There were the smells. The bone beneath. Sweat broke out on me at breakfast. I didn't expect to come home that was not in the plan. Some point I guess the brain cells just give out. You read a hundred military manuals you won't find the word kill they trick you into killing. You get over it it's ok. You have to. Fear not tolerated. Take you out back and shoot you they say. Her eyeglasses in the grass. Standard questionnaire. Fine just say fine. Numb yourself.

Wire-frame. Does it feel good at first yes. Play. Guns. Fire. Animals. You know the Carthaginians liked to use oxen for night fighting. I'm talking about Hannibal I'm talking about the battle of Ager Falernus 217 BC. Like tanks but more frightening. They'd tie lit torches to the horns and stampede them toward the enemy. The Romans panicked some ran into the herd some got knocked off the path to the crags below others tried to retreat and were lost in the tundra never seen again. But what about I'm asking what happens when the torches burn down to the horn to the hair to the head to the bone beneath. So much human cruelty is simply incidental is simply brainless. Simply no common sense. You could take the entirety of the common sense of humans and put it in the palm of your hand and *still have room for your dick.*

YOU SPELL IT number 4
letter *N* letter *O* no space
all caps: 4NO / is it a
nickname / no Babycakes
it's functional the fucking

army being a fucking
fulcrum of fucking
functionality / they called
you 4NO in the army / are

you going to repeat
everything I say / sorry
/ pass the sugar / so you
knew Sad in the army /
indeed I did / he

says you can see the future
you're a prophet / no I see
Seeing I am the god of this
I see Seeing coming /

what's that like / all white
all the time / what do you
mean / I mean the whole
immediate Visible crushed

onto the frontal cortex is
nothing but white without
any Remainder now you'll
say of course there's no

Remainder if a thing hasn't
happened yet! but the
fact is most of what you

people see most of what
you

people call the present
world is just Remainder
just a failure of
Invisibility's flames to
disappear from that

thin edge / a failure / they
were always coming up to
me saying 4NO who'll win
the hockey pool 4NO your

name means Foresight
better get some 4NO
you're the god who knows
the future how come you
got yourself

fuckstuck in this
meatclock didn't you see it
coming / well didn't you /
what I saw coming was
the atomic

essence of the Visible
brought to such a density
its Incandescence left no
place for anyfuckingthing
else /

ah / or am I talking outside
your experiential zipcode /
sort of / give me that sugar
again / so this white stuff's

coming at you all the time
/ yup / you can't stop it / I
can slow it down with
alcohol or pharmaceuticals
I

choose not to / was it
different in the army / hell
yes we were drugged to
the eyeballs / Sad doesn't
talk about

that much / no I bet not /
well he mentioned
something at a crossroads
/ say again / a crossroads a

woman a shopping bag a
white plastic bag I don't
know / here's some advice
/ yes / don't ask about the

woman don't ask about the
crossroads don't ask about
the plastic shopping bag /
okay / don't ask him don't

ask me / okay / time for
my meds I'll leave you
now / it was a pleasure /
oh I doubt that

NO MOON TONIGHT in fact. Ida is watching the room itself. It looks lonely a room needs its work. Once as a child she'd stayed in a department store overnight just to see. She stole nothing. She wanted to understand the way it was with no one watching. She'd brought her drawing book but found it hard to do anything in the dark. She sucks her fingers. His smoky aftertaste. What was it like? he asked after the first sex. Like pie without a fork she said. He smiled. I know about the fork he said. That was their closest moment. It inspired her to step past fear. To believe she had got outside the circle of her mistakes. But then he said you know Ida I'm a man who doesn't like the idea of being liked too much and another night he said love was a big bunch of grass that grows up in your mind and makes you stupid. So much for pie. She leans on her elbow watching Sad and wishing she had her drawing book with her. They are lying on a pile of mattress covers on the floor in weak light from somewhere a night that could so easily not exist. Drawings of Sad so far are minimal. She'd looked at the photos in his wallet and copied one of his father taken the day he dropped his eyeglasses down the well. In the photo he looks younger than Sad is now this father who refused to get another pair of glasses because *I was already seeing too much*. Ida wants to meet the father. Sad is making groaning sounds in his sleep. She touches him. Night's bones are still forming. They get up stiffly and crowd into their clothes and grope across to the big door. Slip out. There against the wall of the corridor sits G with his knees up. Howdy says G.

I AM VERY he says tilting into the room and stops. Happy to see you man but I'm not sure you're real. Tell me you're real. 4NO looks at him upside down then unfolds from his headstand. Bad night? says 4NO. But Sad is straying about the room touching all the chairs one by one. Chairs he says. I missed you. His voice is soft. His eyes drift off. 4NO watches him fragilely. Every molecule of Sad and Sad's bad future is advancing through 4NO's retinal surface. Like perfect works of art they form a sparkling flood. They saturate him and confiscate the present moment. He closes his eyes against this unbearable excess and gathers his mind to a point. It breaks through the white. He opens his eyes. At ease soldier he says to Sad. Nobody's here yet. I'm just stretching. Sad smiles and then forgets not to. The smile stays on his face.

TIME PASSES TIME does not pass. Time all but passes. Time usually passes. Time passing and gazing. Time has no gaze. Time as perseverance. Time as hunger. Time in a natural way. Time when you were six the day a mountain. Mountain time. Time I don't remember. Time for a dog in an alley caught in the beam of your flashlight. Time not a video. Time as paper folded to look like a mountain. Time smeared under the eyes of the miners as they rattle down into the mine. Time if you are bankrupt. Time if you are Prometheus. Time if you are all the little tubes on the roots of a gorse plant sucking greenish black moistures up into new scribbled continents. Time it takes for the postal clerk to apply her lipstick at the back of the post office before the supervisor returns. Time it takes for a cow to tip over. Time in jail. Time as overcoats in a closet.

Time for a herd of turkeys skidding and surprised on ice. All the time that has soaked into the walls here. Time between the little clicks. Time compared to the wild fantastic silence of the stars. Time for the man at the bus stop standing on one leg to tie his shoe. Time taking Night by the hand and trotting off down the road. Time passes oh boy. Time got the jump on me yes it did.

SUE GOYETTE

Ocean

Sue Goyette's *Ocean* is a capacious and ambitious book in which she does no less than re-write the sea and the history of our relationship with it. The individual poems are numbered from one to fifty-six, not named, as is exactly right for the way the book itself ebbs and flows. In *Ocean*, Goyette becomes the spokesperson for a mythical community of shore-dwellers, with the third person "we" in every poem bringing the strength of the collective to the viewpoint, and a refreshing sense of poetry as a communal force rather than an individual plaint. The ocean is its own character — or characters a pet, a starlet, a dragon, a pacing old man. The poems explore the idea of its depth and surfaces, the fear of the under-ocean, the nature and origin of saltiness.

But even though the sea is a constant — sometimes more present, sometimes less, a tidal flow within the poems — Goyette's focus is on the shore. Her interest is in the moving boundary between ocean and land, where the shore-dwellers live. Here is a place of change and myth-making, where transformation happens every day. In *Ocean*, Goyette's vigorous language and large vision create an extraordinary new history of the way the sea has formed human consciousness, shoreline experience, and poetry itself.

One

The real estate agent chewed gum to cover the smell
of bank on his breath and told us a snow fence would keep it

out. That it wasn't so much like student housing
but a wishing well that would one day increase

our property value. Oceanfront was like 24-hour shopping;
we'd browse its surface and wonder who really needed

all this stuff. And what a hurricane of a question!
What a tidal wave of disruption. It got worse

when we walked into it and let it taste us. Courtship!
We had never heard of marriage let alone ceremony.

When we wrote our names in the soft sand of its back,
we didn't know the first thing about commitment

or about being out of our depths.

Four

We first invented running so we could be in two places
at one time but then understood how, with empty pockets,

we could also harvest the wind. We invented hospitality
to lure our successes home, and to get love a much-needed

drink. We invented chairs so we could rest after the chase.
We invented the chase after we invented running, and inadvertently,

robbery. We invented the suburbs after accidentally colliding
into the feud and its conniving stepsisters the argument

and the snit. Some of us needed more space.
We discovered death under the bridge

and someone insisted we take it home, that it needed
our help. That day alone we invented the handkerchief

and the whisper. When it sat up, when it looked at us
with the teeth of its appetite puddinged in its eyes, we discovered

the flapping of words trying to escape from our ears
and something hammering in the silver-shaft of our hearts.

We unearthed fear that day, our first act of real
archeology. Understand, at that point, maps charted roads

and the humble footpaths between rumours crooked
with love. The ocean took up the most room

with its tidal pull and tentacled beasts inventing
their own recipes. Some days we knew we were nothing

but ingredients; other days we felt like honoured guests.
But the day we brushed the dirt from fear's forehead

and got a look at its hands, well, our maps changed
and the ocean got bigger, our nights, a great deal beastier.

Eight

The trick to building houses was making sure
they didn't taste good. The ocean's culinary taste

was growing more sophisticated and occasionally
its appetite was unwieldy. It ate boats and children,

the occasional shoe. Pants. A diamond ring.
Hammers. It ate promises and rants. It snatched up

names like peanuts. We had a squadron of cooks
specifically catering to its needs. They stirred vats

of sandals and sunglasses. They peppered their soups
with pebbles and house keys. Quarts of bottled song

were used to sweeten the brew. Discussions between
preschool children and the poets were added

for nutritional value. These cooks took turns pulling
the cart to the mouth of the harbour. It would take four

of them to shoulder the vat over, tipping the peeled
promises, the baked dreams into its mouth.

And then the ocean would be calm. It would sleep. Our mistake
was thinking we were making it happy.

Eighteen

Some believed the ocean wasn't always salty but that our ancestors
had been very sad. They'd been promised a great many things

only to have the fruit drop and their breasts sag. They cried
a lot. When they looked up and bemoaned their fate,

claiming they'd done nothing to deserve all of this roadkill,
the exhaust from their undeservedness formed a talk show

of rain clouds. When they looked upon the ground
and beseeched their feral happiness to stop chewing

at their feet, their displeasure seeded gout weed and prehistoric
thorned things. In this way, our boats were the original forms

of escape and self-help. At first we floated on our ancestors'
        sadness,
the waters rife with the salt of their tears, but then,

vivre l'evolution, those tears sprouted gills and tails
and small, watchful eyes. It isn't entirely accurate to say

we ate those fish but more like accepted that which we'd inherited.
What we hadn't anticipated was how the eyes of those original
        tears

would persist, how they'd keep watching.

Twenty-Eight

We recruited sturdy lawn chairs and consulted
an architect before placing them on the shore.

Our aim was simple, we wanted to welcome
what the ocean had to tell us and make amends

with it. We wanted the chairs to display our willingness
but also our resolve. We would not be pushed around.

We could only find eight lawn chairs that stood the test
of tide. We advertised it as a master class of listening.

One woman, in response, baked a cake. A carpenter
mailed us a pinecone. We couldn't help but press

the fourth grader's poem about spring to our lips,
tasting the daffodil of its optimism. A miner

sent a flashlight. A mathematician sent a violin.
And a security guard sent his father's cough,

dried like fruit leather. A widow sent her late husband's laugh
distilled into five drops, one for each decade they'd been married.

And an insomniac sent a pillow stuffed with the grass
from the field she no longer dreamt about. Our chairs were filled.

For a long time, the ocean slept. Our fourth grader
insisted he could hear its dreams of swimming trucks

delivering the colour blue and shark fins. There were lights
in its stomach and sometimes, when it heard us, its ears

hurt. The mathematician measured the parabola of his memory
trying to find an equal sign in the ebbing waves.

The security guard had crossed his arms over his chest and
    stood up.
The tide could come in, but only so far. Little flowerets

of his younger self cartwheeled behind him. There was no way
he'd let himself go under again. After allowing a drop

of her late husband's laughter to dissolve on her tongue,
the widow looked long at the ocean. *Bigger*, she said,

much bigger than that. The woman who baked the cake
was on her knees with the miner, icing his resolve to haul up

whatever was buried. The ocean complied by filling in
each hole he'd dug until he realized the treasure he was seeking

was kneeling right there beside him. Between the sunset
and their kiss, we didn't know where to look! The insomniac

didn't want to hear anything above the alarm clock of her heart.
The waves, she claimed, made her feel too rushed. And the
    carpenter,

the carpenter pushed us away when we realized he was crying.
Everything I've ever made, he said, *can float.*

Thirty-Two

We had been feeding thin wafers
of moonlight to our daughters. No one

had warned us of the danger
or the potency of this new fad diet.

But show me a pine tree now and I'll show you
one of our girls. Those cones of persistence;

the sharp needles of argument. Stubborn and green,
green, green. Upward and outward. First they wanted

kittens. Now they want a clean ocean.
They wore their disdain like lip gloss

and flirted with the security cameras
of their fears. Their talk belied their curfews

and they insisted on wearing their grandmothers'
watches. Nothing could make them hurry.

Some of us studied them and now put on
our boots as if every morning is a mountain

not yet tamed. We'd kept our growls on a leash
for so long, when we let them loose they kept looking back

at us. Our girls taught us the right way
to spoon the spilled stars. The infusion

of outer space with the darker oil of our secrets
made us heady with abandon. We fell into the arms

of our daughters as if we'd been lost at sea
and they were the ones standing on shore

to welcome us: grass huts lit with composure.
They'd built a fire, burning everything we had ever

taught them. They had no choice, they explained,
it was the only way they could imagine keeping us warm.

Thirty-Seven

According to our scholars, the newly birthed Milky Way
was rhinestoned with souls, which proved the soul's

existence. The lifeguards, when asked, said they'd tasted
the hard candy of the soul when they tried reviving

an ocean victim. But we'd always been suspicious of souls.
We knew they could escape because we often heard

their hooves, the slap of their tails. They'd wander off
at night and when we'd wake, we'd feel emptier,

our great finned souls swimming against the current
and further away. We'd cover our mouths when we laughed,

when we yawned. Once they broke out, souls were just a nuisance
to coax back. There was a trap of words the poets had sugared

and we'd take classes to learn how to enunciate without sounding
desperate. When they returned, we'd have to swallow our souls

like the pit of a plum or a vitamin. It could take several days
to feel enriched, to see the sky in the puddles again.

Thirty-Eight

Souls became the perfect distraction. We had to keep
their gowns clean. We had to buff their moods.

But some of us were wounded in a way that made our days
need crutches. We were invalids in the pale hospital hours

of our kitchens. No one had warned us that our children
would leave and we were bereft, holding up the bedclothes

of their childhood and breathing deep the pink lambs
of their voice. We had no choice but to steal the poets' trap

of sugared words and meet at the ocean. Bravely, we tried
reciting them without sounding desperate. That our souls

were grazing on the hill behind us no longer mattered.
We wanted to lure our wandering children home.

The words we used had the thin syrup of our loneliness
in their veins. In this way, we learned that words also have souls,

and when the souls of our words escaped, there was a glitter
frosting the ocean, and briefly, we had managed to sugar its tide.

Fifty-Six

Filmmakers had started making films of the ocean
in 3D. Scratch and sniff coastal cards were sold

at lottery booths. Material for dresses was cut with the froth
of tide in mind. We had wanted the ocean to be the new

flavour, the new sound. We'd drive for miles to get a glimpse
of it because, let's face it, it revitalized the part of us

we kept rooting for, that apple seed of energy that defied
multiple choice career options. The ocean had egged the best part

of us on. And it scared us. We never knew what it was thinking
and spent thousands on specialists who could make predictions.

And the predictions always required hard hats and building permits,
furrowed eyebrows and downward trends. Why is it so hard

to trust something that leaps, disappears and then reappears
spouting more light? When had our hearts become badly behaved

dogs we had to keep the screen door closed to? Have you ever run
along its shore, the pant of it coming closer? And that feeling

that yipped inside of you, the Ginger Rogers of your feet, your ability
to not get caught then, yes, get soaked. Didn't you feel like it was

part of your pack? When it whistled, whatever it is in you
that defies being named, didn't that part of you perk up?

And didn't you let it tousle you to the ground,
let it clean between your ears before it left you?

Wasn't that all right? That it left you? That we all will?

ANNE MICHAELS

Correspondences

Anne Michaels' *Correspondences* is a single, intensely lyrical poem of something over 700 lines, in 54 unnumbered sections. With an exceedingly spare vocabulary and a voice as light as a whisper, the poem weaves recollections of Paul Celan, Nelly Sachs, and many others into an elegy for the author's father, Isaiah Michaels. The text is accompanied by reproductions of 26 gouache portraits by Bernice Eisenstein, and the physical book is designed and constructed in such a way that the portraits are subtly privileged over the text. In effect, the poem is hidden on the underside of the paintings. Yet the poem, for all its modesty, attempts something momentous.

It is a sustained interrogation of language, memory, history, sunlight, and rain in search of words that are simple and clean enough to speak, as Michaels says, from someplace "deeper than a single heart." It is a search for a language not only the living but also "the dead might understand and trust." And it is an exercise in learning to read from and write on a highly elusive surface: the hidden place that Michaels calls the third side of the page.

The wet earth. I did not imagine
your death would reconcile me with
language, did not imagine soil
clinging to the page, black type
like birds on a stone sky. That your soul — yes,
I use that word — beautiful,
could saturate the bitterness from even
that fate, not of love
but its opposite, all concealed
in a reversal of longing.

They wanted you to shout *oranges*
in the street, a few coins from the grocer
to raise your voice. But you stared
at the pyramid of perfume and oil,
and instinctively smelled your fingers
for the vanished scent, and felt into
your pocket for the bit of peel carried
since. And stood,
the mud of another country
still on your shoes. Silenced
by that bit of earth.
While Celan in Paris wept
for the same contraband,
ronger and *grincer*
gnawing and grinding
between *voix* and *voie*
voice and path,
between converse and its converse
between Ancel and Celan
between Mayer and Amery
between the Nemen and the Prut
between the Prut and the Seine
between *sauf* and *soif,*
rescue and
thirst.

The scribe speaks aloud each word
as he writes,
wipes clean the quill
and bathes himself entire,
>   *Woman washes woman,*
>   *man washes man*
before writing His name.
>   *in the water's flow,*
>   *never turn the face*
>   *from the sky,*
The holy ink is ritually prepared:
tannic acid, crystals of iron sulfate,
ground gallnut.
>   *the body must never be alone,*
>   *never so vulnerable the soul*
>   *as when first*
>   *separate*
No two letters
may touch each other.
>   *not from the moment of death*
>   *to the moment of burial,*
>   *not while the soul still hovers*
From the top of each line,
>   *one fringe of the prayer shawl must be cut away*
each letter is suspended.
>   *for that shawl will not be used anymore for prayer*
>   *in life*
please understand
>   *ich bin mit meinem selbst allein*
No page bearing His name
may be discarded.
>   *vater father, wasser water*
A holy book

you must wash the body and
the soul guarding the body
must be buried.
with water and with prayer

The same question endlessly repeated,
fingers grasping the same crumbling edge,
one of the first signs of illness
never allowing a lesion to form.
How to cope financially, how to make
nothing into something. When I was still a child
you asked my brothers and I to sit with you
at the table; *I implore you,*
it is all I ask: do what you love, only
choose work you love, no matter what it is.
Not like me, making nothing
out of nothing. Though at least you came out ahead
on one side of the ledger, the side of love dark
with pencil marks, the black of my mother's hair
as she sat in the row ahead at the concert hall
the night you met. Unlike me, with both
blank pages. *How are you coping*, you asked,
over and over, *financially.*
The dreaded endless question born of worry and
helplessness. At least, I always joked, when
you have nothing, nothing can be taken from you,
but we both knew that was bad math, that there was
always something to be taken from you,
not lost, but taken. And so that was the one question
on which you alighted, in the last months
before that decade of silence,
an endless painful longing to rescue,
the repetition of the plough horse,
majestic head bent to earth,
turning the same direction
at the end of each row.

Not only what a soul remembers
but all it forgets,

as if all you know and all you don't know
have changed places;

cloud shadow on the hills,
the sudden downpour in the vale of Borrowdale,
turning the blue slate black,
bare arms in the rain;
animals turned to stone in the blue lias beds;
the name that can't be understood
without its story;
the narrow-bladed paddle and
all the water it displaces;
the help and helplessness
of love;

the photos and the millions
of indifferent eyes that have looked upon
their shaven nakedness;

the ghost life that lives itself
beside us, the shadow of what happened
and what didn't happen;

If ever I lose
my memory of you, walk beside me
like a stag; like a bird heard, unseen

The scribe writes a language
without vowels, the reader's breath
   Celan read the river, his Seine
   sein, his
must not be represented,
must remain invisible,
each word
   eine, one
   keine, no,
   none
an oxygen tent, a shelter
of consonants,
   water, a will rushing
breath to set fire
   heaven, it is written, is a seine
   thrown into the sea
to meaning
   as the seine draws in, a breath, we swim
   toward the net, not away
the difference between end *and*
and,
   as the *sein*, being, belonging to,
   draws near
soiled *and*
solid,
   draw
men *and*
mein
   me in,
   mein

Sometimes we are led through the doorway
by a child, sometimes
by a stranger, always a matter of grace changing
the past, for if there is anything we must change
it is the past. To look back
and see another map.

Love enough to fill
a shoe, a suitcase, a bit of ink,
a painting, a child's eyes at a chalkboard,
a bit of chalk, a bit of
bone in ash.

All that is cupped,
all that is emptied

the rush of water from a pump,
a word spelled out
on a palm.

their relationship to their bodies changed,
bone, not flesh, containing the soul

and when the natural order of flesh
was restored, the place the soul was stored
was not;

too much
soul left in the bone

enough to fill
a bit of light on the water

To name the world
that contains this world
the way night and morning
are the same day

or like the moment of
looking into that face and finding
yourself suddenly or was it slowly
alone,
who is that woman with the baby,
pointing to me and to your grandchild

and when your language ceased,
a gap ever widening, swaying and closing, swaying and
opening between us, every word with the
inarticulation of the sea when there is
no shore to break and therefore bring
its rhythm, the swaying deck from which you
reached out to that coffin, to that child,

I began the piling of words,
to dig myself out
to dare myself
that single word

the buried book,
the typewritten record, the handwritten
witnessing,

the precise waking that is born
from the nightmare,

and so,
I beg you,

come out of the night, just this night, and into
the hallway,

leave your boots
by the door, where they will be safe

here in the room of the lit window
you saw from the street,
each to smell their favourite dish
each to hear his own language,
her own song, mother and father
tongue, mother and father
reading under the lamp, the lost child
asleep upstairs, the lover's breast,
the mother's breast, the book open

to the third side of the page

ABOUT THE POETS

RACHAEL BOAST was born in Suffolk in 1975. Her first collection of poetry, *Sidereal*, won the Forward Prize for Best First Collection and the Seamus Heaney Prize in 2012. She is editor of *The Echoing Gallery: Bristol Poets and Art in the City* and deputy director of the Bristol Poetry Institute. She currently divides her time between Scotland and the West Country.

ANNE CARSON was born in Canada and has been a professor of Classics for more than thirty years. She was twice a finalist for the National Book Critics Circle Award; was honoured with the 1996 Lannan Award and the 1997 Pushcart Prize, both for poetry; and was named a MacArthur Fellow in 2000. In 2001 she received the T. S. Eliot Prize for Poetry, the 2001 Griffin Poetry Prize, and the *Los Angeles Times* Book Prize. She currently teaches at the University of Michigan and lives in Ann Arbor.

SUE GOYETTE has published three collections of poetry and a novel, *Lures*. She has won the Pat Lowther Memorial Award, the Atlantic Poetry Prize, the CBC Literary Prize for Poetry, the Earle Birney Prize, the Bliss Carman Award, and has been shortlisted for the Governor General's Literary Award. She lives in Halifax, Nova Scotia, where she teaches creative writing and works part-time at the Writers' Federation of Nova Scotia.

BRENDA HILLMAN has published nine collections of poetry, including *Practical Water*, which won the *Los Angeles Times* Book

Prize for Poetry and *Seasonal Works with Letters on Fire,* which was longlisted for the National Book Award. Hillman has received fellowships from the National Endowment for the Arts and the Guggenheim Foundation, two Pushcart Prizes, a Holloway Fellowship from the University of California at Berkeley, and the Delmore Schwartz Memorial Award for Poetry. Hillman serves as a professor and poet-in-residence at St. Mary's College in Morago, California. She is also a member of the permanent faculties of Squaw Valley Community of Writers and Napa Valley Writers' Conference.

ANNE MICHAELS is the author of three poetry collections, including *The Weight of Oranges,* which won the Commonwealth Prize for the Americas, and *Miner's Pond,* which received the Canadian Authors Association Award and was shortlisted for the Governor General's Literary Award and the Trillium Award. Her novel *Fugitive Pieces* won the Lannan Literary Award for Fiction, the Chapters/*Books in Canada* First Novel Award, the *Guardian* Fiction Award, and the Orange Prize for Fiction. Her second novel, *The Winter Vault,* was a finalist for the Scotiabank Giller Prize, the Trillium Book Award, and the Commonwealth Writers' Prize. Her work has been translated into more than thirty languages.

CARL PHILLIPS is the author of twelve books of poetry, including *Speak Low,* which was a finalist for the National Book Award, and *Double Shadow,* also a finalist for the National Book Award and winner of the *Los Angeles Times* Book Prize. He has received numerous awards and honours, including the Kingsley Tufts Poetry Award, the Theodore Roethke Memorial Foundation Award in Poetry, a Lambda Book Award, and the Thom Gunn Award for Best Gay Male Poetry, as well as fellowships from the Academy of American Poets, the American Academy of Arts and Letters, the Guggenheim Foundation, and the Library of Congress. Phillips was elected a Chancellor of the Academy of American Poets in 2006. He teaches at Washington University, in St. Louis, Missouri.

MIRA ROSENTHAL's first book, *The Local World*, won the Wick Poetry Prize in 2011. She is the translator of two volumes of poetry by Tomasz Różycki, most recently *Colonies*, which received the PEN Translation Fund Award. Among her awards are fellowships from the National Endowment for the Arts, the MacDowell Colony, the American Council of Learned Societies, and Stanford University, where she was a Wallace Stegner Fellow in Poetry. Her poems, translations, and essays have been published in many journals and anthologies, including *Ploughshares*, *American Poetry Review*, *Harvard Review*, *Slate*, *PN Review*, *A Public Space*, and *Mentor and Muse: Essays from Poets to Poets*.

TOMASZ RÓŻYCKI is a poet, critic, and translator. He has published nine books, including the Koscielski Prize–winning epic poem *Dwanascie Stacji* (*Twelve Stations*) and the sonnet cycle *Kolonie* (*Colonies*), both of which were nominated for Poland's most prestigious literary award, the NIKE. His awards include the Josif Brodski Prize, the Czechowicz Poetry Prize, the Rainer Maria Rilke Prize, and the 3 Quarks Daily Prize in Arts and Literature. His work has been translated into English, French, Slovak, Italian, German, and Serbian. He lives in the Silesian city of Opole in southwestern Poland with his wife and two children.

ABOUT THE JUDGES

ROBERT BRINGHURST has published some twenty books of poetry. He has been a Guggenheim Fellow in poetry and has held research grants in Native American literature and linguistics from the Social Sciences and Humanities Research Council of Canada, the Centre National de la Recherche Scientifique (Paris), and the American Philosophical Society, Philadelphia. He held the Atwood-Roy chair in Canadian Literature at the Universidad Nacional Autónoma de México in 2008. In 2010, he served as Distinguished Writer in Residence at the University of Wyoming and in 2011 as Witter Bynner fellow in poetry at the Library of Congress. In 2013, he was appointed an Officer of the Order of Canada.

JO SHAPCOTT was born in London, England. Poems from her three award-winning collections, *Electroplating the Baby*, *Phrase Book*, and *My Life Asleep* are gathered in a selected poems, *Her Book*. She has won a number of literary prizes including the Commonwealth Writers' Prize for Best First Collection, the Forward Prize for Best Collection and the National Poetry Competition (twice). *Tender Taxes*, her versions of Rilke, was published in 2001. Her most recent collection, *Of Mutability*, was published in 2010 and won the Costa Book Award. In 2011 Jo Shapcott was awarded the Queen's Gold Medal for Poetry.

C. D. WRIGHT is the author of more than a dozen books, most recently, *One With Others: a little book of her days*, which won the National Book Critics Circle Award and the Lenore Marshall Prize and was a finalist for the National Book Award. A limited edition of her long poem *Breathtaken* with linocuts by Walter Feldman was published by Ziggurat in 2012. Her book *Rising, Falling, Hovering* won the 2009 Griffin Poetry Prize. With photographer Deborah Luster she published *One Big Self: Prisoners of Louisiana* that won the Lange-Taylor Prize from the Center for Documentary Studies at Duke University. On a fellowship for writers from the Wallace Foundation she curated a "Walk-in Book of Arkansas," a multi-media exhibition that toured throughout her native state. She teaches at Brown University and lives outside of Providence, Rhode Island.

ACKNOWLEDGEMENTS

The publisher thanks the following for their kind permission to reprint the work contained in this volume:

"Caritas," "Cocteau Twins," "Losing My Page," "The Withdrawing Room," "After Sappho," "Milestones," "Aubade," "Tearing and Mending," "Redressing Marsyas," and "Spring Tide" from *Pilgrim's Flower* by Rachael Boast are reprinted by permission of Picador.

Selections from *Red Doc>* by Anne Carson are reprinted by permission of Jonathan Cape and McClelland & Stewart.

"One," "Four," "Eight," "Eighteen," "Twenty-Eight," "Thirty-Two," "Thirty-Seven," "Thirty-Eight," and "Fifty-Six" from *Ocean* by Sue Goyette are reprinted by permission of Gaspereau Press.

"At the Solstice, a Yellow Fragment," "Between Semesters, the Fragments Follow Us," "Equinox Ritual with Ravens & Pines," "To Leon, Born before a Marathon," "Fable of Work in the World," "Very Far Back in This Life," "To the Writing Students at Orientation," "When the Occupations Have Just Begun," "& the Tents Went Back Up," "An Almanac of Coastal Winter Creatures," "The Second Half of the Survey," and "In the Evening of the Search," from *Seasonal Works with Letters on Fire* by Brenda Hillman are reprinted by permission of Wesleyan University Press.

Selections from *Correspondences* by Anne Michaels are reprinted by permission of McClelland & Stewart.

"Just the Wind for a Sound, Softly," "Now Rough, Now Gentle," "Flight of Doves," "Surrounded as We Are, Unlit, Unshadowed," "First You Must Cover Your Face," "Black Swan on Water, in a Little Rain," "My Meadow, My Twilight," "The Difference between Power and Force," "Darkness Is as Darkness Does," "Shimmer," "Anyone Who Had a Heart," and "But Waves, They Scatter" from *Silverchest* by Carl Phillips are reprinted by permission of Farrar, Straus and Giroux.

"Creoles, Mestizos / *Kreole, metysi*," "The Storm / *Burza*," "Headwinds / *Przeciwne wiatry*," "Coral Bay / *Koralowa zatoka*," "Shamans / *Szamani*," "*L'intérieur / Interior*," "Scorched Maps / *Spalone mapy*," "Old Fortress / *Stara twierdza*," "Cannibals / *Ludożercy*," "Opium / *Opium*," "Dolphins / *Delfiny*," and "The Governor's Residence / *Dom gubernatora*" from *Colonies* by Tomasz Różycki, translated by Mira Rosenthal, are reprinted by permission of Zephyr Press.

THE 2014 GRIFFIN POETRY PRIZE ANTHOLOGY

The best books of poetry published in English internationally and in Canada are honoured each year with the $65,000 Griffin Poetry Prize, one of the world's most prestigious and valuable literary awards. Since 2001 this annual prize has acted as a tremendous spur to interest in and recognition of poetry, focusing worldwide attention on the formidable talent of poets writing in English. Each year the editor of *The Griffin Poetry Prize Anthology* gathers the work of the extraordinary poets shortlisted for the awards and introduces us to some of the finest poems in their collections.

This year, editor and prize juror Robert Bringhurst's selections from the international shortlist include poems from Rachael Boast's *Pilgrim's Flower* (Picador), Brenda Hillman's *Seasonal Works with Letters on Fire* (Wesleyan University Press), Carl Phillips' *Silverchest* (Farrar, Straus and Giroux), and Tomasz Różycki's *Colonies* (Zephyr), translated by Mira Rosenthal. The selections from the Canadian shortlist include selections from Anne Carson's *Red Doc>* (Jonathan Cape and McClelland & Stewart), *Ocean* by Sue Goyette (Gaspereau Press), and *Correspondences* by Anne Michaels (McClelland & Stewart).

In choosing the 2014 shortlist, prize jurors Robert Bringhurst, Jo Shapcott, and C. D. Wright considered 539 collections published in the previous year. The jury also wrote the citations that introduce the seven poets' nominated works. Royalties generated from

The 2014 Griffin Poetry Prize Anthology will be donated to UNESCO's World Poetry Day, which was created to support linguistic diversity through poetic expression and to offer endangered languages the opportunity to be heard in their communities.

The Griffin Trust